JANUARY

2005	2006	2007	2008	2009
1	1 2 3 4 5 6 7	1 2 3 4 5 6	1 2 3 4 5	1 2 3
2 3 4 5 6 7 8	8 9 10 11 12 13 14	7 8 9 10 11 12 13	6 7 8 9 10 11 12	4 5 6 7 8 9 10
9 10 11 12 13 14 15	15 16 17 18 19 20 21	14 15 16 17 18 19 20	13 14 15 16 17 18 19	11 12 13 14 15 16 17
16 17 18 19 20 21 22	22 23 24 25 26 27 28	21 22 23 24 25 26 27	20 21 22 23 24 25 26	18 19 20 21 22 23 24
23 24 25 26 27 28 29	29 30 31	28 29 30 31	27 28 29 30 31	25 26 27 28 29 30 31
30 31				

1 _____
2 _____
3 _____
4 _____
5 _____
6 _____
7 _____
8 _____
9 _____
10 _____

11 _____
12 _____
13 _____
14 _____
15 _____
16 _____
17 _____
18 _____
19 _____
20 _____

21 _____
22 _____
23 _____
24 _____
25 _____
26 _____
27 _____
28 _____
29 _____
30 _____
31 _____

Notes

Sweet Valentine

Love is all around! Wear your heart on your sleeve — or your ankle.

Size Women's medium

Planned finished measurements: foot length 9½", foot circumference 8" when stretched slightly, leg length 6½"

Materials

300 yds of sport weight yarn

2.75 mm/US 2 ndls **or size required** to obtain **gauge of 7½ sts/inch** over stockinette

For socks as pictured use Lorna's Laces Shepherd Sport (70g/200 yds), 2 skeins Sherbet #801

Also see Beaded Sweet Valentine variation in Appendix

Instructions (make 2)

Cast on 62 sts. Join, placing mkr for eor.

Work 1" of cuff ribbing: *(k2, p2) 3 times, k2, p1, (k3, p1) 4 times*

Work **Ribbing and Hearts Panel** rnds 1 – 14 four times for 56 rnds total.

Reposition eor to side of sock: remove mkr, (k2, p2) 3 times, k2, p1, k8, replace mkr.

Next 3 rnds: k7, p1, (k2, p2) 3 times, k2, p1, k15, p1, (k2, p2) 3 times, k2, p1, k8.

Setup for 29 st heel: (k1, sl 1) 7 times, k2tog, (sl 1, k1) 7 times.

Place remaining 32 sts on hold for instep.

Referring to Appendix, work Round Heel. Staying in established pattern on instep sts, dec gussets to 62 total foot sts.

Continue foot in established pattern until sock measures 7½" from back of heel, or 2" shorter than overall foot length desired.

Referring to Appendix, work Wedge Toe until 18 sts remain.

Ribbing and Hearts Panel (31 st multiple, 14 rnd rep)

Rnd 1: *(k2, p2) 3 times, k2, p1, k2, yo, ssk, k7, k2tog, yo, k2, p1*

All even-numbered rnds: *(k2, p2) 3 times, k2, p1, k15, p1*

Rnd 3: *(k2, p2) 3 times, k2, p1, k3, yo, ssk, k5, k2tog, yo, k3, p1*

Rnd 5: *(k2, p2) 3 times, k2, p1, k2, yo, ssk, yo, ssk, k3, k2tog, yo, k2tog, yo, k2, p1*

Rnd 7: *(k2, p2) 3 times, k2, p1, k3, yo, ssk, yo, ssk, k1, k2tog, yo, k2tog, yo, k3, p1*

Rnd 9: *(k2, p2) 3 times, k2, p1, k4, yo, ssk, yo, sl 1, k2tog, psso, yo, k2tog, yo, k4, p1*

Rnd 11: *(k2, p2) 3 times, k2, p1, k1,(k1, k2tog, yo, k1, yo, ssk) 2 times, k2, p1*

Rnd 13: *(k2, p2) 3 times, k2, p1, k1, k2tog, yo, k3, yo, sl 1, k2tog, psso, yo, k3, yo, ssk, k1, p1*

First of All, Have Fun!

Welcome to the The Sock Journal: Knit the Year in Socks, the second collection in The Sock Calendar series.

As in our first book, we've built options into The Sock Journal patterns to give you opportunities for lots of creative variety, and hope this will encourage you to try new things.

Each pattern has stitch and design appeal that is not dependent on the yarn used in the photo. For example, where a variegated yarn is shown, try a solid color for an attractive variation. And vice versa.

We offer interchangeable instructions for two heel styles and two toe styles that you can mix and match. So, if the featured sock is photographed with a Round Heel and Wedge Toe, you might try it with a Peasant Heel and Spiral Toe.

For easy and fun knitted embellishments, check out January's beaded Renaissance socks (be forewarned that beading is totally addictive!) and September's embroidered Varsity Sox.

We'd love to hear from you and please let us know what you'd like to see included in the next collection. We welcome you to visit and participate in our cyberlist and online photo gallery hosted at the HeartStrings FiberArts web site.

Sizes Given in Patterns

As there is no single standard for sock-sizing, we have provided both commonly-used size designations and finished measurements for each pattern. Several of the designs have unisex appeal and would make handsome socks for men or women.

In all instances, you should check the measurements given in the pattern against the foot measurements of the prospective wearer and adjust accordingly. It is easy to increase a few stitches for a wider intended foot or work a longer foot before shaping the toe.

If you want to make a sock in a size not provided, refer to the sock's pattern stitch multiple for easy recalculation. As a reference, for foot length, you can use September's Varsity Sox which is given in a range of sizes from child's small to adult extra large.

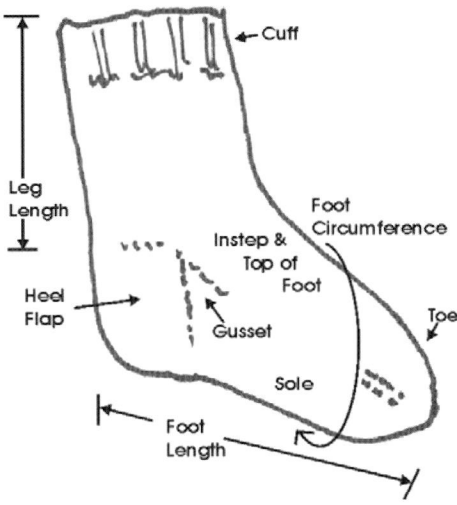

Yarns and Yardage

We specifically designed the patterns to be knitable using widely-available yarns. While we've indicated the yarns used in the photo, we encourage you to explore alternatives, also. On the inside back cover, there is an informative Yarns Used substitution matrix that lists all the pertinent data.

We provided yardage for each pattern based on the sizes indicated and yarns pictured. When adjusting size or substituting other yarns, err on the side of caution and plan for more if you are at all in doubt. We've even found that yardage can vary by color, dyelot and other variables. And gauge! Which brings us to…

Gauge

We know that you know that gauge is critical. So we won't belabor it beyond reminding you to check your gauge for accuracy. If the gauge doesn't match that for the pattern, change needles accordingly.

Needles

The patterns are not dependent on any one style of needles. Use your preference for knitting on sets of 4 or 5 double points, two circulars, or a single circular. The important things are to get the correct gauge and be comfortable.

Waste Yarn

The Peasant Heel instructions require that you knit heel stitches onto waste yarn before completing the foot. [We also prefer to put inactive stitches on waste yarn when working the Round Heel to avoid straining the instep edge stitches.] The ideal waste yarn is slippery and thinner than the working yarn for easy removal later. It is also in a color that contrasts with the working yarn for the same reason. Some knitters prefer to use embroidery floss as their perfect waste yarn, while others use whatever skinny yarn is at hand.

Finishing

We don't have sock-specific ideas beyond warning you, for comfort reasons, to avoid any knots in the sock. So remember to leave longish 3 – 4" ends that can be securely woven in on the inside of the sock.

Wash according to your yarn's care instructions. Block or not as you desire.

        Wear and enjoy!

Renaissance

Begin an elegant and shining new year with beaded diamonds from another time and place.

Size   Women's medium

Planned finished measurements: foot length 9½", foot circumference 8", leg length 6½"

Materials

350 yds of fingering weight yarn

2.75 mm/US 2 ndls or size required to obtain **gauge of 8 sts/inch** over stockinette

816 size 8/0 (3 mm) seed beads

Small sewing or tapestry ndl for stringing beads

For socks as pictured use Brown Sheep Wildfoote (50g/215 yds), 2 balls Bluegrass SY-400; Miyuki 8/0 seed beads, 25g Galvanized Silver #1051

sl bead-p1 – slide a bead into place next to ndl, then p1, taking care that the bead remains at front of work and is not pulled through the loop when completing the p stitch

Instructions (make 2)

Using ndl for stringing beads, string 408 beads onto yarn. As you knit, slide beads down along the yarn until needed.

Cast on 64 sts. Join, placing mkr for eor.

Work 1¼" of cuff ribbing: *k2, p2*

Knit 1 rnd.

Work **Beaded Border** rnds 1 – 6.

Work **Beaded Diamonds** rnds 1 – 8 six times, then rnds 1 – 6 once more for 54 rnds total.

Knit 3 rnds.

Setup for 31 st heel: (k1, sl 1) 15 times, k1.

Place remaining 33 sts on hold for instep.

Referring to Appendix, work Round Heel. Dec gussets to 64 total foot sts.

Continue foot in stockinette until sock measures 7½" from back of heel, or 2" shorter than overall foot length desired.

Referring to Appendix, work Spiral Toe.

Beaded Border
(8 st multiple, 6 rnds)

Rnd 1: *sl bead-p1, k1*

Rnds 2, 4, 6: knit

Rnd 3: *k1, sl bead-p1*

Rnd 5: *k2, (sl bead-p1, k1) 3 times*

Beaded Diamonds
(8 st multiple, 8 rnd rep)

Rnd 1: *k4, sl bead-p1, k3*

Rnds 2, 4, 6, 8: knit

Rnd 3: *k2, sl bead-p1, k3, sl bead-p1, k1*

Rnd 5: *sl bead-p1, k7*

Rnd 7: rep rnd 3

FEBRUARY

2005	2006	2007	2008	2009
1 2 3 4 5 6 7 8 9 10 11 12 13 14 15 16 17 18 19 20 21 22 23 24 25 26 27 28	1 2 3 4 5 6 7 8 9 10 11 12 13 14 15 16 17 18 19 20 21 22 23 24 25 26 27 28	1 2 3 4 5 6 7 8 9 10 11 12 13 14 15 16 17 18 19 20 21 22 23 24 25 26 27 28	1 2 3 4 5 6 7 8 9 10 11 12 13 14 15 16 17 18 19 20 21 22 23 24 25 26 27 28 29	1 2 3 4 5 6 7 8 9 10 11 12 13 14 15 16 17 18 19 20 21 22 23 24 25 26 27 28

1 _____
2 _____
3 _____
4 _____
5 _____
6 _____
7 _____
8 _____
9 _____
10 _____

11 _____
12 _____
13 _____
14 _____
15 _____
16 _____
17 _____
18 _____
19 _____
20 _____

21 _____
22 _____
23 _____
24 _____
25 _____
26 _____
27 _____
28 _____
29 _____

Notes

O'Socks

In honor of ancient Celtic designs and just in time for St. Patrick's Day.

Size Women's medium

Planned finished measurements: foot length 9½", foot circumference 8", leg length 5½"

Materials

300 yds of sport weight yarn

3.25 mm/US 3 ndls or size required to obtain **gauge of 6½ sts/inch** over stockinette

Cable needle (CN)

For socks as pictured use Gems Opal (50g/112 yds), 3 skeins Teal #54

Celtic Knot
(32 st multiple, 16 rnd rep)

Rnd 1: *k3, p3, C4B, (p4, C4B) 2 times, p3, k3*

Rnd 2: *k3, p3, k4, (p4, k4) 2 times, p3, k3*

Rnd 3: *k3, p2, T3B, (T4F, T4B) 2 times, T3F, p2, k3*

Rnd 4: *k3, p2, k2, p3, k4, p4, k4, p3, k2, p2, k3*

Rnd 5: *k3, p1, T3B, p3, C4F, p4, C4F, p3, T3F, p1, k3*

Rnd 6: *k3, p1, k2, p4, (k4, p4) 2 times, k2, p1, k3*

Rnd 7: *k3, p1, k2, p3, T3B, T4F, T4B, T3F, p3, k2, p1, k3*

Rnd 8: *k3, p1, (k2, p3) 2 times, k4, (p3, k2) 2 times, p1, k3*

Rnd 9: *k3, p1, (k2, p3) 2 times, C4B, (p3, k2) 2 times, p1, k3*

Rnd 10: rep rnd 8

Rnd 11: *k3, p1, k2, p3, T3F, T4B, T4F, T3B, p3, k2, p1, k3*

Rnd 12: rep rnd 6

Rnd 13: *k3, p1, T3F, p3, C4F, p4, C4F, p3, T3B, p1, k3*

Rnd 14: rep rnd 4

Rnd 15: *k3, p2, T3F, (T4B, T4F) 2 times, T3B, p2, k3*

Rnd 16: rep rnd 2

C4B (Cable 4 Back) – sl 2 onto CN and hold to back of work, k2, k2 from CN

C4F (Cable 4 Front) – sl 2 onto CN and hold to front of work, k2, k2 from CN

T3B (Twist 3 Back) – sl 1 onto CN and hold to back of work, k2, p1 from CN

T3F (Twist 3 Front) – sl 2 onto CN and hold to front of work, p1, k2 from CN

T4B (Twist 4 Back) – sl 2 onto CN and hold to back of work, k2, p2 from CN

T4F (Twist 4 Front) – sl 2 onto CN and hold to front of work, p2, k2 from CN

Instructions (make 2)

Cast on 56 sts. Join, placing mkr for eor.

Work 1" of cuff ribbing: *p2, k2*

Inc rnd: *(k1-inc) 2 times, p4, (k2, p2) 4 times, k2, p1, p1-inc, k1, k1-inc* (64 sts)

Work **Celtic Knot** rnds 1 – 16 two times, then rnds 1 – 10 once more for 42 rnds total.

Dec rnd: *k3, p1, (ssk, p3) 2 times, ssk, k2tog, (p3, k2tog) 2 times, p1, k3* (52 sts)

Knit 1 rnd.

Setup for 25 st heel: (k1, sl 1) 6 times, k2tog, (sl 1, k1) 6 times.

Place remaining 26 sts on hold for instep.

Referring to Appendix, work Round Heel. Dec gussets to 52 total foot sts.

Continue foot in stockinette until sock measures 7½" from back of heel, or 2" shorter than overall foot length desired.

Referring to Appendix, work Spiral Toe.

MARCH

2005	2006	2007	2008	2009
1 2 3 4 5 6 7 8 9 10 11 12 13 14 15 16 17 18 19 20 21 22 23 24 25 26 27 28 29 30 31	1 2 3 4 5 6 7 8 9 10 11 12 13 14 15 16 17 18 19 20 21 22 23 24 25 26 27 28 29 30 31	1 2 3 4 5 6 7 8 9 10 11 12 13 14 15 16 17 18 19 20 21 22 23 24 25 26 27 28 29 30 31	1 2 3 4 5 6 7 8 9 10 11 12 13 14 15 16 17 18 19 20 21 22 23 24 25 26 27 28 29 30 31	1 2 3 4 5 6 7 8 9 10 11 12 13 14 15 16 17 18 19 20 21 22 23 24 25 26 27 28 29 30 31

1 _____
2 _____
3 _____
4 _____
5 _____
6 _____
7 _____
8 _____
9 _____
10 _____

11 _____
12 _____
13 _____
14 _____
15 _____
16 _____
17 _____
18 _____
19 _____
20 _____

21 _____
22 _____
23 _____
24 _____
25 _____
26 _____
27 _____
28 _____
29 _____
30 _____
31 _____

Notes

On the Avenue

Spring marks the beginning of strolling season. Get ready with handsome new socks for you and yours.

Sizes [Adult S, M/L, L/XL]

Planned finished measurements:
 foot length [8½, 10, 11½]"
 foot circumference [7¼, 8½, 9¾]"
 leg length [5¾, 7, 8]"

Materials

Sport weight yarn:
 [250, 325, 400] yds of Main Color (MC)
 [15, 18, 20] yds of Alternate Color(s) (AC)

2.75 mm/US 2 ndls <u>or size required</u> to obtain **gauge of 7¾ sts/inch** over stockinette

3.25 mm/US 3 ndls or one size larger than those used to obtain gauge

For socks as pictured use Dale of Norway Tiur (50g/126 yds):

 To left (S) – 2 balls yellow #2304, 1 ball blue #5834
 To right (L/XL) – 4 balls gray #5041, 1 ball each yellow #2304 and blue #5834

Instructions (make 2)

With smaller ndls and your choice of MC or AC, cast on [56, 66, 76] sts. Join, placing mkr for eor.

With MC, work [1, 1¼, 1¾]" cuff in your choice of ribbing.
For gray man's sock: *k1, p1*
For yellow woman's sock: *k2, p2*

Change to larger ndls.

Work **Textured Dots** rnds 1 – 12 [4, 5, 6] times, then rnds 1 – 6 [1, 1, 0] more time for [54, 66, 72] rnds total.

Continue in MC only.

Knit 3 rnds.

Change to smaller ndls.

Setup for [29, 33, 37] st heel: (k1, sl 1) [14, 16, 18] times, k1.

Place remaining [27, 33, 39] sts on hold for instep.

Referring to Appendix, work Round Heel. Dec gussets to [56, 66, 76] total foot sts.

Continue foot in stockinette until sock measures [6¾, 8, 9¼]" from back of heel, or [1¾, 2, 2¼]" shorter than overall foot length desired.

Referring to Appendix, work your choice of Wedge Toe (as for yellow sock) until [16, 18, 20] sts remain, or Spiral Toe (as for gray sock).

Textured Dots
(2 st multiple, 12 rnd rep)

Rnd 1 – 4 (use MC): knit

Rnd 5 (use AC): *k1, sl 1*

Rnd 6 (use AC): *p1, sl 1*

Rnd 7 – 10 (use MC): knit

Rnd 11 (use AC): *sl 1, k1*

Rnd 12 (use AC): *sl 1, p1*

APRIL

2005	2006	2007	2008	2009
1 2 3 4 5 6 7 8 9 10 11 12 13 14 15 16 17 18 19 20 21 22 23 24 25 26 27 28 29 30	1 2 3 4 5 6 7 8 9 10 11 12 13 14 15 16 17 18 19 20 21 22 23 24 25 26 27 28 29 30	1 2 3 4 5 6 7 8 9 10 11 12 13 14 15 16 17 18 19 20 21 22 23 24 25 26 27 28 29 30	1 2 3 4 5 6 7 8 9 10 11 12 13 14 15 16 17 18 19 20 21 22 23 24 25 26 27 28 29 30	1 2 3 4 5 6 7 8 9 10 11 12 13 14 15 16 17 18 19 20 21 22 23 24 25 26 27 28 29 30

1 _____

2 _____

3 _____

4 _____

5 _____

6 _____

7 _____

8 _____

9 _____

10 _____

11 _____

12 _____

13 _____

14 _____

15 _____

16 _____

17 _____

18 _____

19 _____

20 _____

21 _____

22 _____

23 _____

24 _____

25 _____

26 _____

27 _____

28 _____

29 _____

30 _____

Notes

Mother & Child

Every mother and baby deserves a gift knitted with love. Here's a set of pretty, matching socks to please.

Sizes Women's medium [newborn/infant]

Planned finished measurements:
foot length 9½ [3¼]"
foot circumference 8 [4½]"
leg length 5 [2½]"

Materials

300 [75] yds of sport weight yarn

2.75 mm/US 2 ndls or size required to obtain **gauge of 7½ sts/inch** over stockinette

2.25 mm/US 1 ndls or one size smaller than those used to obtain gauge

Ribbon

For a set of Mother's Socks and Baby Booties as pictured use Ornaghi Filati Bebé Layette (150g/490 yds), 1 ball color #31

TieBow – look at next st and follow it down 8 rnds, insert ndl into front of the st in that rnd (the middle st of the 9 purled sts) and draw yarn loop through it, placing the loop on LHN; k2tog the loop and next st

Mother's Socks Instructions
(make 2)

With larger ndls, cast on 60 sts. Join, placing mkr for eor.

Work 1" of cuff ribbing: *k2, p2*

Eyelet rnd: *k1, k2tog, yo, k2*

Knit 4 rnds.

Work **Bowties** rnds 1 – 30, then rnds 1 – 15 once more for 45 rnds total.

Setup for 29 st heel: (k1, sl 1) 7 times, k2tog, (sl 1, k1) 7 times.

Place remaining 30 sts on hold for instep.

Referring to Appendix, work Round Heel. Dec gussets to 60 total foot sts.

Continue foot in stockinette until sock measures 7½" from back of heel, or 2" shorter than overall foot length desired.

Referring to Appendix, work Spiral Toe.

Baby Booties Instructions
(make 2)

With smaller ndls, cast on 36 sts. Join, placing mkr for eor.

Work ¾" of cuff ribbing: *k2, p2*

Change to larger ndls.

Eyelet rnd: *k4, k2tog, yo*

Knit 4 rnds.

Place a single Bowtie motif on the front of the bootie as follows.

Rnds 1 – 2: k22, p9, k5.

Rnds 3 – 6: knit

Rnds 7 – 8: rep rnds 1 – 2.

Rnd 9: k26, TieBow, k9.

Knit 6 rnds.

Setup for 19 st heel: (k1, sl 1) 9 times, k1.

Place remaining 17 sts on hold for instep.

Referring to Appendix, work Round Heel to depth of ¾". Dec gussets to 36 total foot sts.

Continue foot in stockinette until sock measures 2¼" from back of heel, or 1¼" shorter than overall foot length desired.

Referring to Appendix, work Spiral Toe.

MAY

| 2005 | 2006 | 2007 | 2008 | 2009 |

1 _____
2 _____
3 _____
4 _____
5 _____
6 _____
7 _____
8 _____
9 _____
10 _____

11 _____
12 _____
13 _____
14 _____
15 _____
16 _____
17 _____
18 _____
19 _____
20 _____

21 _____
22 _____
23 _____
24 _____
25 _____
26 _____
27 _____
28 _____
29 _____
30 _____
31 _____

Notes

Bowties (15 st multiple, 30 rnd rep)
Rnds 1 – 2: *k3, p9, k3*
Rnds 3 – 6: knit
Rnds 7 – 8: rep rnds 1 – 2
Rnd 9: *k7, TieBow, k7*
Rnds 10 – 15: knit
Rnds 16 – 17: *p4, k6, p5*
Rnds 18 – 21: knit
Rnds 22 – 23: rep rnds 16 – 17
Rnd 24: *k14, TieBow*
Rnds 25 – 30: knit

Promise

"Something old, something new ... " and something pretty.

Size   Women's medium

Planned finished measurements: foot length 9½", foot circumference 8" when stretched slightly, leg length 5½"

Materials

300 yds of fingering weight yarn

2.75 mm/US 2 ndls <u>or size required</u> to obtain **gauge of 8 sts/inch** over stockinette

3.25 mm/US 3 ndls or one size larger than those used to obtain gauge

Cable needle (CN)

Waste yarn

For socks as pictured use Dale of Norway Baby Ull (50g/190 yds), 2 balls color #5726

C2B (Cable 2 Back) – sl 1 onto CN and hold to back of work, k1, k1 from CN

T2B (Twist 2 Back) – sl 1 onto CN and hold to back of work, k1, p1 from CN

T2F (Twist 2 Front) – sl 1 onto CN and hold to front of work, p1, k1 from CN

Instructions (make 2)

With larger ndls, cast on 64 sts. Join, placing mkr for eor.

Work **Cathedral Windows** rnds 1 – 14 four times for 56 rnds total.

Reposition eor to side of sock: remove mkr, k2, replace mkr.

Change to smaller ndls.

Next 4 rnds: k33, p1, work Cathedral Windows as established over next 28 sts, p1, k1.

Heel placement: k32 using waste yarn to mark where Peasant Heel will be worked later. Return waste yarn sts to LHN and reknit them using the working yarn.

Continue foot in established pattern until sock measures 5½" from back of heel, or 4" shorter than overall foot length desired.

Referring to Appendix, work Wedge Toe until 20 sts remain and Peasant Heel until 28 sts.

Cathedral Windows
(4 st multiple, 14 rnd rep)

Rnds 1 – 6: *k1, p2, k1*

Rnd 7: *T2F, T2B*

Rnd 8: *p1, k2, p1*

Rnd 9: *p1, C2B, p1*

Rnd 10: *p1, k2, p1*

Rnd 11: *T2B, T2F*

Rnds 12 – 14: *k1, p2, k1*

JUNE

2005	2006	2007	2008	2009
1 2 3 4 5 6 7 8 9 10 11 12 13 14 15 16 17 18 19 20 21 22 23 24 25 26 27 28 29 30	1 2 3 4 5 6 7 8 9 10 11 12 13 14 15 16 17 18 19 20 21 22 23 24 25 26 27 28 29 30	1 2 3 4 5 6 7 8 9 10 11 12 13 14 15 16 17 18 19 20 21 22 23 24 25 26 27 28 29 30	1 2 3 4 5 6 7 8 9 10 11 12 13 14 15 16 17 18 19 20 21 22 23 24 25 26 27 28 29 30	1 2 3 4 5 6 7 8 9 10 11 12 13 14 15 16 17 18 19 20 21 22 23 24 25 26 27 28 29 30

1 _____
2 _____
3 _____
4 _____
5 _____
6 _____
7 _____
8 _____
9 _____
10 _____

11 _____
12 _____
13 _____
14 _____
15 _____
16 _____
17 _____
18 _____
19 _____
20 _____

21 _____
22 _____
23 _____
24 _____
25 _____
26 _____
27 _____
28 _____
29 _____
30 _____

Notes

Carnival

Did someone say Rio? Here are tropically-inspired socks to have you dancing on the beach!

Sizes [Women's S, M, L]
Planned finished measurements:
   foot length [9, 9½, 10½]"
   foot circumference [7½, 8, 9]"
   leg length [5½, 6, 6½]"

Materials

300 [325, 350] yds of fingering weight yarn

2.25 mm/US 1 ndls <u>or size required</u> to obtain **gauge of 8 sts/inch** over stockinette

Cable needle (CN)

For women's medium socks as pictured use Lorna's Laces Shepherd Sock (2 oz/215 yds), 2 skeins Sweetie #222

Instructions (make 2)

Cast on [60, 64, 72] sts. Join, placing mkr for eor.

Work 1" of cuff ribbing: *k2, p2*

Knit 1 rnd, evenly increasing [0, 2, 0] sts. ([60, 66, 72] sts)

Knit [2, 5, 8] rnds.

Work **Carnival Stitch** rnds 1 – 11 five times, then rnds 1 – 2 once more for 46 rnds total.

Knit [2, 5, 8] rnds.

Knit 1 rnd, evenly decreasing [0, 2, 0] sts. ([60, 64, 72] sts)

Setup for [29, 31, 35] st heel: (k1, sl 1) [14, 15, 17] times, k1.

Place remaining [31, 33, 37] sts on hold for instep.

Referring to Appendix, work Round Heel. Dec gussets to [60, 64, 72] total foot sts.

Carnival Stitch (6 st multiple, 11 rnd rep)

Rnd 1: *k1 wrapping yarn twice loosely around ndl in the process (instead of the usual once)*

Rnd 2: *sl 3 to CN (dropping the extra wraps to make elongated loops) and hold to back of work, p3 (dropping the extra wraps to make elongated loops), p3 from CN*

Rnds 3 – 11: knit

Continue foot in stockinette until sock measures [7, 7½, 8½]" from back of heel, or 2" shorter than overall foot length desired.

Referring to Appendix, work Wedge Toe until [16, 20, 24] sts remain.

JULY

2005	2006	2007	2008	2009
1 2 3 4 5 6 7 8 9 10 11 12 13 14 15 16 17 18 19 20 21 22 23 24 25 26 27 28 29 30 31	1 2 3 4 5 6 7 8 9 10 11 12 13 14 15 16 17 18 19 20 21 22 23 24 25 26 27 28 29 30 31	1 2 3 4 5 6 7 8 9 10 11 12 13 14 15 16 17 18 19 20 21 22 23 24 25 26 27 28 29 30 31	1 2 3 4 5 6 7 8 9 10 11 12 13 14 15 16 17 18 19 20 21 22 23 24 25 26 27 28 29 30 31	1 2 3 4 5 6 7 8 9 10 11 12 13 14 15 16 17 18 19 20 21 22 23 24 25 26 27 28 29 30 31

1 _____
2 _____
3 _____
4 _____
5 _____
6 _____
7 _____
8 _____
9 _____
10 _____

11 _____
12 _____
13 _____
14 _____
15 _____
16 _____
17 _____
18 _____
19 _____
20 _____

21 _____
22 _____
23 _____
24 _____
25 _____
26 _____
27 _____
28 _____
29 _____
30 _____
31 _____

Notes

Coolers

Summer heat doesn't stop the knitter! Try these quick, air-conditioned short socks.

Size Women's medium

Planned finished measurements: foot length 9½", foot circumference 8", leg length 3½"

Materials

275 yds of fingering weight yarn

2.25 mm/US 1 ndls <u>or size required</u> to obtain **gauge of 9 sts/inch** over stockinette

For women's socks as pictured (left) use Lang Jawoll Jacquard Superwash (45g/207 yds), 2 balls color #159

Below: Stitch pattern knitted in Lang Jawoll Superwash color #43

Instructions (make 2)

Cast on 72 sts. Join, placing mkr for eor.

Work 1" of cuff ribbing: *k2, p2*

Knit 3 rnds.

Work **Lozenge Stitch** rnds 1 – 20.

Work in stockinette until sock measures 3½" from cast on.

Setup for 35 st heel: (k1, sl 1) 17 times, k1.

Place remaining 37 sts on hold for instep.

Referring to Appendix, work Round Heel. Dec gussets to 72 total foot sts.

Continue foot in stockinette until sock measures 7½" from back of heel, or 2" shorter than overall foot length desired.

Referring to Appendix, work Spiral Toe.

Lozenge Stitch
(8 st multiple, 20 rnds)

Rnd 1: purl

Rnds 2 – 3: knit

Rnd 4: purl

Rnds 5, 7, 9, 11, 13, 15: knit

Rnd 6: *k3, yo, ssk, k3*

Rnd 8: *k2, (yo, ssk) 2 times, k2*

Rnd 10: *k1, (yo, ssk) 3 times, k1*

Rnd 12: rep rnd 8

Rnd 14: rep rnd 6

Rnd 16: knit

Rnd 17: purl

Rnds 18 – 19: knit

Rnd 20: purl

AUGUST

2005	2006	2007	2008	2009
1 2 3 4 5 6	1 2 3 4 5	1 2 3 4	1 2	1
7 8 9 10 11 12 13	6 7 8 9 10 11 12	5 6 7 8 9 10 11	3 4 5 6 7 8 9	2 3 4 5 6 7 8
14 15 16 17 18 19 20	13 14 15 16 17 18 19	12 13 14 15 16 17 18	10 11 12 13 14 15 16	9 10 11 12 13 14 15
21 22 23 24 25 26 27	20 21 22 23 24 25 26	19 20 21 22 23 24 25	17 18 19 20 21 22 23	16 17 18 19 20 21 22
28 29 30 31	27 28 29 30 31	26 27 28 29 30 31	24 25 26 27 28 29 30	23 24 25 26 27 28 29
			31	30 31

1 _____
2 _____
3 _____
4 _____
5 _____
6 _____
7 _____
8 _____
9 _____
10 _____

11 _____
12 _____
13 _____
14 _____
15 _____
16 _____
17 _____
18 _____
19 _____
20 _____

21 _____
22 _____
23 _____
24 _____
25 _____
26 _____
27 _____
28 _____
29 _____
30 _____
31 _____

Notes

Varsity Sox

Rah, rah, sis boom bah! Support your favorite team by wearing their colors.

Sizes [Child S, M, L] [Adult S, M, M/L, L, XL]
Planned finished measurements:
   foot length [5½, 6¾, 7¾] [8½, 9½, 10¼, 11, 12]"
   foot circumference [5, 5¾, 6½] [7¼, 8, 8½, 9¼, 10]"
   leg length [3¾, 4, 4½] [5, 5½, 6¼, 7, 7½]"

Materials
[110, 140, 175] [225, 275, 325, 380, 440] yds of sport weight yarn in your choice of color(s)

3.25 mm/US 3 ndls <u>or size required</u> to obtain **gauge of 7 sts/inch** over stockinette

Waste yarn (if doing Peasant Heel version)

Optional: Yarn for embroidered letter

For socks as pictured use Brown Sheep Nature Spun Sport (50g/184 yds):

   Team letter version (in adult S) — 2 balls Impasse Yellow #305, small amount of Blue Knight #N04

   Unlettered version with contrast heels/toes (in adult S) — 2 balls Touche Teal #N05, 1 ball Natural #730

   Striped leg version (child M) — 1 ball each Orange You Glad #008 and Turquoise Wonder #019

Instructions (make 2)

Cast on [35, 40, 45] [50, 55, 60, 65, 70] sts. Join, placing marker for eor.

Work **Beaded Rib** rnds 1 – 2 until sock measures approx [¾, ¾, 1] [1¾, 1½, 1¾, 2, 2]" <u>and completing</u> rnd 2. Note: for striped version, alternate colors every 7 rnds.

Optional Framed Insert for Letter
(area inside frame is 13 sts by 19 rnds)

Frame rnd: p15, *k1, p1, k1, p2*

Insert rnd 1: k13, p2, *k3, p2*

Insert rnd 2: k13, p2, *k1, p1, k1, p2*

Rep Insert rnds 1 – 2 eight more times, then rnd 1 once more. Work Frame rnd once more.

Continue in Beaded Rib as established until sock measures [3¾, 4, 4½] [5, 5½, 6¼, 7, 7½]" from cast on.

Knit 1 rnd.

To position framed insert either at side or front of leg (your choice): remove mkr, k to the position which will become the ankle side seam just before start of heel.

Complete socks using your choice of heel and toe styles. See Appendix for Peasant Heel/Wedge Toe version (as shown to left in photo), or proceed below to work Round Heel/Spiral Toe version (to right in photo).

Setup for [17, 21, 23] [25, 27, 29, 31, 35] st round heel: (k1, sl 1) [8, 10, 11] [12, 13, 14, 15, 17] times, k1.

Place next [18, 19, 22] [25, 28, 31, 34, 35] sts on hold for instep. Remaining [17, 21, 23] [25, 27, 29, 31, 35] sts will be worked for heel.

Referring to Appendix, work Round Heel flap. Note: Before turning heel, work heel flap to [1½, 1¾, 2] [2, 2¼, 2¼, 2½, 2¾]" or desired heel depth. Dec gussets to [34, 40, 46] [50, 56, 60, 64, 70] total foot sts.

Continue foot in stockinette until sock measures [4¼, 5¼, 6¼] [6¾, 7½, 8¼, 8¾, 9½]" from back of heel, or [1¼, 1½, 1½] [1¾, 2, 2, 2¼, 2½]" shorter than overall foot length desired.

Referring to Appendix, work Spiral Toe.

Referring to Appendix, embroider optional team letter.

Beaded Rib
(5 st multiple, 2 rnd rep)

Rnd 1: *k1, p1, k1, p2*

Rnd 2: *k3, p2*

SEPTEMBER

2005	2006	2007	2008	2009
1 2 3	1 2	1	1 2 3 4 5 6	1 2 3 4 5
4 5 6 7 8 9 10	3 4 5 6 7 8 9	2 3 4 5 6 7 8	7 8 9 10 11 12 13	6 7 8 9 10 11 12
11 12 13 14 15 16 17	10 11 12 13 14 15 16	9 10 11 12 13 14 15	14 15 16 17 18 19 20	13 14 15 16 17 18 19
18 19 20 21 22 23 24	17 18 19 20 21 22 23	16 17 18 19 20 21 22	21 22 23 24 25 26 27	20 21 22 23 24 25 26
25 26 27 28 29 30	24 25 26 27 28 29 30	23 24 25 26 27 28 29	28 29 30	27 28 29 30
		30		

1 _____
2 _____
3 _____
4 _____
5 _____
6 _____
7 _____
8 _____
9 _____
10 _____
11 _____
12 _____
13 _____
14 _____
15 _____
16 _____
17 _____
18 _____
19 _____
20 _____
21 _____
22 _____
23 _____
24 _____
25 _____
26 _____
27 _____
28 _____
29 _____
30 _____

Notes

Cobblestone

A comfortable walking sock inspired by memories of Beacon Hill.

Size   Adult medium

Planned finished measurements: foot length 9½", foot circumference 8", leg length 5½"

Materials

350 yds of sport weight yarn

2.75 mm/US 2 ndls <u>or size required</u> to obtain **gauge of 7½ sts/inch** over stockinette

2.25 mm/US 1 ndls or one size smaller than those used to obtain gauge

For socks as pictured use Mountain Colors Bearfoot (100g/350 yds), 1 skein Wild Raspberry

Instructions (make 2)

With smaller ndls, cast on 64 sts. Join, placing mkr for eor.

Work 1" of cuff ribbing: *k2, p2*

Inc rnd: (k2, p2) 8 times, m1, (k2, p2) 8 times, m1. (66 sts)

Change to larger ndls.

Knit 2 rnds.

Work **Cobblestone Stitch** rnds 1 – 16 four times for 64 rnds total.

Setup for 33 st heel: (k1, sl 1) 16 times, k1.

Place remaining 33 sts on hold for instep.

Referring to Appendix, work Round Heel. Staying in established pattern on instep sts, dec gussets to 66 total foot sts.

Continue foot in established pattern until sock measures 7½" from back of heel, or 2" shorter than overall foot length desired.

Referring to Appendix, work Wedge Toe until 18 sts remain.

Cobblestone Stitch
(6 st multiple, 16 rnd rep)

Note: Slip all sts with yarn held to back of work.

Rnd 1: *k4, sl 1, k1*

Rnds 2 – 4: *p4, sl 1, p1*

Rnds 5 – 8: knit

Rnd 9: *k1, sl 1, k4*

Rnds 10 – 12: *p1, sl 1, p4*

Rnds 13 – 16: knit

OCTOBER

2005	2006	2007	2008	2009
1	1 2 3 4 5 6 7	1 2 3 4 5 6	1 2 3 4	1 2 3
2 3 4 5 6 7 8	8 9 10 11 12 13 14	7 8 9 10 11 12 13	5 6 7 8 9 10 11	4 5 6 7 8 9 10
9 10 11 12 13 14 15	15 16 17 18 19 20 21	14 15 16 17 18 19 20	12 13 14 15 16 17 18	11 12 13 14 15 16 17
16 17 18 19 20 21 22	22 23 24 25 26 27 28	21 22 23 24 25 26 27	19 20 21 22 23 24 25	18 19 20 21 22 23 24
23 24 25 26 27 28 29	29 30 31	28 29 30 31	26 27 28 29 30 31	25 26 27 28 29 30 31
30 31				

1 _____
2 _____
3 _____
4 _____
5 _____
6 _____
7 _____
8 _____
9 _____
10 _____

11 _____
12 _____
13 _____
14 _____
15 _____
16 _____
17 _____
18 _____
19 _____
20 _____

21 _____
22 _____
23 _____
24 _____
25 _____
26 _____
27 _____
28 _____
29 _____
30 _____
31 _____

Notes

Tenderfoot

Remember Jack Frost, hayrides and new slipper sox every winter? Continue the tradition with these comfy, all-knitted ones.

Size   Adult medium

Planned finished measurements: foot length 9½", foot circumference 8", leg length 5½"

Materials

300 yds of DK weight yarn

3.5 mm/US 4 ndls <u>or size required</u> to obtain **gauge of 6½ sts/inch** over stockinette

For socks as pictured use Garnstudio Karisma (50g/120 yds), 3 balls color #8

Instructions (make 2)

Cast on 52 sts. Join, placing mkr for eor.

Work 1" of cuff ribbing: *k2, p2*

Knit 5 rnds.

Work **Moire** rnds 1 – 9 three times, then rnds 1 – 8 once more for 35 rnds total.

Inc rnd: k26, (k6, k1-inc, k6) 2 times. (54 sts)

Work rnd 1 of **Moire** across next 26 sts, and place these sts on hold for instep. Work remaining 28 sts in **THS** until heel flap measures approx 2" or desired length, <u>and completing</u> through a WS row.

Heel turn row 1 (RS): k15, ssk, k1, turn work.

Heel turn row 2 (WS): sl 1 wyib, k1, sl 1 wyib, k1, k2tog, k1, turn.

Heel turn row 3 (RS): sl 1 wyib, k to 1 st before last st worked on prev row, then ssk this st with next unworked st, k1, turn.

Heel turn row 4 (WS): sl 1 wyib, *k1, sl 1 wyib; rep from * to last st worked on prev row, k2tog this st with the next unworked st, k1, turn.

Rep Heel turn rows 3 – 4 until all sts have been incorporated, and remembering to stay in pattern as established. (16 sts remain)

Cut yarn, leaving a tail to weave in later. Re-attach yarn at beginning of instep sts. K across instep sts, place gusset mkr #1, pick up and k an even number of sts along edge of heel flap, k across heel flap sts, pick up and k the same number of sts along other edge of heel flap, place gusset mkr #2 which will also serve as the eor mkr.

The sock will now be worked in Moire on the instep/foot sts starting with Moire rnd 3, and an in-the-round version of THS on the sole.

Gusset rnd 1: work **Moire** across instep sts, sl mkr #1, p2, *sl 1 wyif, p1; rep from * to eor mkr.

Gusset rnd 2: work **Moire** across instep sts, sl mkr #1, k2tog, k to 2 sts before eor mkr, ssk.

Rep Gusset rnds 1 – 2 until 56 sts remain.

Continue as established in **Moire** across instep/foot sts and **TSS** across sole sts until sock measures 7½" from back of heel or 2" less than overall length desired, <u>and completing</u> Rnd 2 or Rnd 4 of TSS.

Referring to Appendix, work Wedge Toe staying in pattern as established, until 20 sts remain.

Moire
(2 st multiple, 9 rnd rep)
Rnd 1: *sl 1 wyib, k1, yo, pass sl st over knit st <u>and</u> yo*
Rnd 2: knit
Rnd 3: rep rnd 1
Rnds 4 – 9: knit

NOVEMBER

2005	2006	2007	2008	2009
1 2 3 4 5 6 7 8 9 10 11 12 13 14 15 16 17 18 19 20 21 22 23 24 25 26 27 28 29 30	1 2 3 4 5 6 7 8 9 10 11 12 13 14 15 16 17 18 19 20 21 22 23 24 25 26 27 28 29 30	1 2 3 4 5 6 7 8 9 10 11 12 13 14 15 16 17 18 19 20 21 22 23 24 25 26 27 28 29 30	1 2 3 4 5 6 7 8 9 10 11 12 13 14 15 16 17 18 19 20 21 22 23 24 25 26 27 28 29 30	1 2 3 4 5 6 7 8 9 10 11 12 13 14 15 16 17 18 19 20 21 22 23 24 25 26 27 28 29 30

1 _____
2 _____
3 _____
4 _____
5 _____
6 _____
7 _____
8 _____
9 _____
10 _____

11 _____
12 _____
13 _____
14 _____
15 _____
16 _____
17 _____
18 _____
19 _____
20 _____

21 _____
22 _____
23 _____
24 _____
25 _____
26 _____
27 _____
28 _____
29 _____
30 _____

Notes

Tenderfoot Heel Stitch (THS) (2 st multiple, 4 row rep)
Note: This stitch is worked back and forth in rows
Rows 1 and 3 (RS): knit
Row 2: *k1, sl 1 wyib; rep from * to last 2 sts, k2
Row 4: k2, *sl 1 wyib, k1*

Tenderfoot Sole Stitch (TSS) (2 st multiple, 4 rnd rep)
Note: This stitch is worked in the rnd across the sole sts only
Rnds 1 and 3: knit
Rnd 2: p2, *sl 1 wyif, p1*
Rnd 4: *p1, sl 1 wyif; rep from * to last 2 sts, p2

Hearth & Tree

Deck the halls with boughs of holly and sockfuls of good cheer!

Sizes Holiday Stocking [Ornament]
Planned finished measurements: foot length 9 [3]", foot circumference 12 [4]", leg length 14 [2¼]"

Materials for Holiday Stocking

240 yds of heavy worsted weight yarn

5 mm/US 8 ndls or size required to obtain **gauge of 4½ sts/inch** over stockinette

7.5 mm/US 7 ndls or one size smaller than those used to obtain gauge

For stocking as pictured use Heirloom EasyCare 12 (50g/72 yds), 4 balls color #705

Materials for Mini-sock Ornament

35 yds of fingering weight yarn

2.75 mm/US 2 ndls or size required to obtain **gauge of 8 sts/inch** over stockinette

For ornament as pictured use Heirloom Baby Wool (25g/98 yds), 1 ball color #404

C3B – Cable 3 Back; sl 2 onto CN and hold to back of work, k1, k2 from CN

C6B – Cable 6 Back; sl 3 onto CN and hold to back of work, work 3 sts in established pattern, work 3 sts in established pattern from CN

C6F – Cable 6 Front; sl 3 onto CN and hold to front of work, work 3 sts in established pattern, work 3 sts in established pattern from CN

Stocking Instructions

With smaller ndls, cast on 63 sts. Join, placing mkr for eor.

Work **Cabled Ribbing** rnds 1 – 4 twice, then rnds 1 – 2 once more for 10 rnds total.

Change to larger ndls.

Work **Wreath Cable** rnds 1 – 20 four times, then rnds 1 – 4 once more for 84 rnds total.

Setup for 27 st heel: m1, (sl 1, k1) 13 times.

Place remaining 37 sts on hold for instep.

Referring to Appendix, work Round Heel to depth of 2½". Staying in established pattern on instep sts, dec gussets to 62 total foot sts.

Continue foot in established pattern until sock measures approximately 7" from back of heel <u>and completing</u> through rnd 17 of Wreath Cable.

Referring to Appendix, work Wedge Toe until 42 sts remain.

Hanging Loop (optional): With smaller ndls, cast on 3 sts. *k3, slide sts across ndl, tug yarn snugly; rep from * until cord measures 3½". Bind off. Fold cord in half and sew to stocking at center back of cuff.

Ornament - See Appendix.

Cabled Ribbing
(21 st multiple, 4 rnd rep)
Rnd 1: *k3, p3, k3, p2, k2, p2, k3, p3*
Rnd 2: *C3B, p3, k3, p2, k2, p2, k3, p3*
Rnds 3 – 4: rep rnds 1 – 2

Seed (2 st multiple, 2 rnd rep)
Rnd 1: *k1, p1*
Rnd 2: *p1, k1*

Wreath Cable
(21 st multiple, 20 rnd rep)
Rnds 1 – 4: *k3, p3, k3, work 6 sts in Seed, k3, p3*
Rnd 5: *C3B, p3, C6B, C6F, p3*
Rnds 6 – 9: *k3, p3, work 3 sts in Seed, k6, work 3 sts in Seed, p3*
Rnd 10: *C3B, p3, work 3 sts in Seed, k6, work 3 sts in Seed, p3*
Rnds 11 – 14: rep rnds 6 – 9
Rnd 15: *C3B, p3, C6F, C6B, p3*
Rnds 16 – 19: rep rnds 1 – 4
Rnd 20: *C3B, p3, k3, work 6 sts in Seed, k3, p3*

DECEMBER

2005	2006	2007	2008	2009
1 2 3	1 2	1	1 2 3 4 5 6	1 2 3 4 5
4 5 6 7 8 9 10	3 4 5 6 7 8 9	2 3 4 5 6 7 8	7 8 9 10 11 12 13	6 7 8 9 10 11 12
11 12 13 14 15 16 17	10 11 12 13 14 15 16	9 10 11 12 13 14 15	14 15 16 17 18 19 20	13 14 15 16 17 18 19
18 19 20 21 22 23 24	17 18 19 20 21 22 23	16 17 18 19 20 21 22	21 22 23 24 25 26 27	20 21 22 23 24 25 26
25 26 27 28 29 30 31	24 25 26 27 28 29 30	23 24 25 26 27 28 29	28 29 30 31	27 28 29 30 31
	31	30 31		

1 _____
2 _____
3 _____
4 _____
5 _____
6 _____
7 _____
8 _____
9 _____
10 _____

11 _____
12 _____
13 _____
14 _____
15 _____
16 _____
17 _____
18 _____
19 _____
20 _____

21 _____
22 _____
23 _____
24 _____
25 _____
26 _____
27 _____
28 _____
29 _____
30 _____
31 _____

Notes

APPENDIX

WEDGE TOE

To set up for working toe, redistribute total sts on ndls so that half are on one ndl (for the top of the foot), and the remaining sts on another. Place mkr at end of each ndl, then redistribute sts on 3 – 4 ndls. K to nearest mkr (now called the eor mkr; the other mkr will be called the middle-of-rnd mkr).

Rnd 1: k1, k2tog, k to 3 sts before middle-of-rnd mkr, SSK, k2, k2tog, k to 3 sts before eor mkr, SSK, k1. (4 sts dec)

Rnd 2: knit.

Rep these 2 rnds until number of toe sts remain as indicated in your pattern. Refer to CLOSING THE TOE AND HEEL and finish toe.

SPIRAL TOE

The spiral toe is worked on any multiple of 6 sts.

Setup rnd: knit, decreasing evenly around to a multiple of 6 sts if necessary.

Knit 4 rnds in stockinette.

Re-arrange sts so that there are the same number of sts on each of 3 ndls. Mark half-way point on each ndl.

Rnd 1: (k to 2 sts from half-way mkr, k2tog, k to 2 sts from end of ndl, k2tog) 3 times. (6 sts dec)

Rnd 2: knit.

Rep rnds 1 - 2 until 18 sts remain. Rep rnd 1 only until 6 sts remain.

Cut yarn leaving approx an 8" tail and thread a tapestry needle. Run yarn through remaining sts twice. Remove sts from knitting ndls and snug up the opening. Bring yarn end through to inside of sock.

Note: For the second sock, you can optionally reverse the direction of the spiral for a mirror-image look. Substitute Rnd 1a below for Rnd 1 in the prev instructions.

Rnd 1a: (ssk, k to half-way mkr, ssk, k to end of ndl) 3 times. (6 sts dec)

ROUND HEEL

Heel Flap Remove eor mkr, as you will now be working back and forth in rows on the heel flap sts only. To begin, turn so WS faces you.

Row 1 (WS): purl.

Row 2 (RS): * k1, sl 1; rep from * to last st, k1.

Rep rows 1 - 2 until heel flap measures depth desired and completing through a WS row. *Note: 2¼" for adult medium sizes, depth indicated in pattern for other sizes, or your own measurement.*

Turn Heel *Short row 1* (RS): k to center st and knit it, then k1, ssk, k1, turn work.

Short row 2 (WS): sl 1 wyif, p4, p2tog, p1, turn.

Short row 3 (RS): sl 1 wyib, k to last st worked on prev row, then ssk this st with the next unworked st, k1, turn.

Short row 4 (WS): sl 1 wyif, p to last st worked on prev row, then p2tog this st with the next unworked st, p1, turn.

Rep short rows 3 – 4 until all sts have been incorporated.

Note: The last time that short rows 3 and 4 can be worked before incorporating all sts, there may be only one unworked st at each end of the ndl. Thus, just work to the last 2 sts of each row and ssk or p2tog as established, then turn work.

Gussets With RS facing you, sl 1 wyib, k across remaining heel sts. Resume working in the rnd as follows. Pick up and k 1 st approx every other row along side of heel flap, place mkr #1, staying in established pattern work across instep sts, place mkr #2, pick up and k same number of sts along other edge of heel flap as the first, k to mkr #1.

Tip: Each slipped st along length of heel flap, worked on the even-numbered rows, represents 2 rows so is an easy benchmark. Thus pick up 1 st for every slipped st, plus any extra required for a neat edge.

The tidiest way to pick up the stitches is to insert working needle between the slipped st and the last (knitted or purled) st of that row. The "pick-ups" will tuck nicely under the adjacent slipped sts for a clean, gap-free edge.

Gusset rnd 1: Work even in pattern as established, ending 2 sts before mkr #1.

Gusset rnd 2: ssk, sl mkr #1, work instep sts as established, sl mkr #2, k2tog, work to mkr #1. (2 sts dec)

Rep gusset rnds 1 - 2 until your pattern's designated number of total foot sts remains. Remove mkr #2, leaving eor mkr #1 in place for eor.

PEASANT HEEL

Notice that the waste yarn is holding the loops for sts that you re-knitted for heel placement.

Carefully remove the waste yarn while putting the released st loops from the ankle part of the sock onto one ndl A, and the ones from the sole onto another ndl C. *Note: There will be one more loop on ndl C than on ndl A.*

Move approx last ½ of sts off ndl A onto a third ndl B. Move 1 st at end of ndl C to ndl A, and move 1 st at other end of ndl C to ndl B.

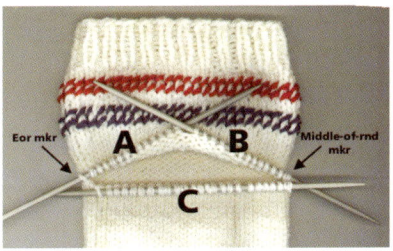

Note: The red/white/blue sock used as an example in the above picture is Yankee Doodle, the July pattern in The Sock Calendar: Socks for All Seasons.

Set-up rnd Join yarn at beg of ndl A. Place eor mkr, k2tog snugly, k across ndls A and B to last 2 sts before end of B, ssk snugly, place middle-of-rnd mkr. Knit approx halfway across ndl C, m1, k across remainder of ndl C to eor mkr. (there are now an equal number of sts between the 2 mkrs)

Knit 2 rnds.

After this initial set-up, the heel shaping is the same as for the Wedge Toe and thus familiar to work. Rep rnds 1 and 2 as in Wedge Toe instructions until number of heel sts remain as indicated in your sock pattern. Refer to CLOSING THE TOE AND HEEL and finish heel.

Note: Because a new yarn is joined to work the heel, the heel is easy to replace if worn out and won't easily unravel in the process – simply remove the worn yarn and rework rnds 1 and 2.

CLOSING THE TOE AND HEEL

Here are instructions for either of two methods you may use to close the Wedge Toe and Peasant Heel.

The *Kitchener Stitch* method will produce a seamless join. Or you can turn the sock inside out, taking care that sts do not fall off ndls, and work a *3-Needle Bind Off* for an easy seamed join.

Preparation for both Kitchener Stitch and 3-Needle Bind Off

Cut yarn, leaving a 12 – 18" end. Thread yarn end into a tapestry ndl. Arrange sts to be joined, so that top of foot sts are on one ndl, and remaining sts on another ndl. With sts to be joined on the 2 separate ndls, hold ndls parallel in same hand so that one ndl is in front of the other with ndl points to the right, and yarn end is coming off to the right.

Kitchener Stitch

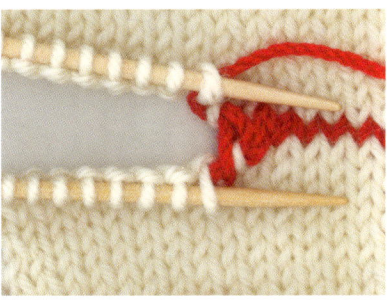

Notes: Remember to bring yarn under ndls when moving between ndls. Adjust tension of sewn sts as necessary to match knitted fabric.

BEGIN by "sewing" with tapestry ndl into first on front ndl as if to purl; then "sew" into first st on back ndl as if to knit.

Rep the following 4 steps until only the last st remains on each of the front and back ndls.

On front ndl

1. "sew" into first st as to knit, sl this st off ndl

2. "sew" into second st as to purl

On back ndl

3. "sew" into first st as to purl, sl this st off ndl

4. "sew" into second st as to knit

END by working steps 1 and 3 only. Bring yarn end through to inside of sock.

3-Needle Bind Off

Using a 3rd ndl: Insert ndl as if to knit through st on front ndl and st on back ndl, k these 2 sts tog. *k2tog front and back ndl sts again, pass previously completed st on

RHN over the k2tog st just made; rep from * across ndls until end. Bring yarn end through last st made.

VARSITY SOX

Continuation of Peasant Heel/ Wedge Toe version —

k [17, 21, 23] [25, 27, 29, 31, 35] using waste yarn to mark where Peasant Heel will be worked later. Return waste yarn sts to LHN and reknit them using the working yarn.

Continue foot in stockinette until sock measures [3, 3¾, 4½] [5, 5½, 6, 6½, 7]" from back of heel, or [2½, 3, 3¼] [3½, 4, 4¼, 4½, 5]" shorter than overall foot length desired.

Optionally, attach contrast color yarn. Work Wedge Toe until [10, 12, 14] [18, 20, 20, 20, 22] sts remain.

Optionally, attach contrast color yarn. Work Peasant Heel until [14, 18, 18] [22, 26, 26, 30, 30] sts remain.

VARSITY TEAM LETTER EMBROIDERY

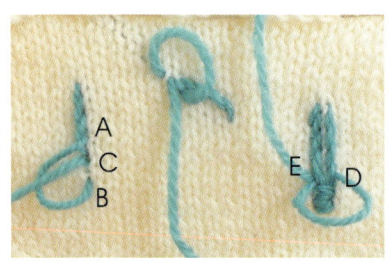

Decide upon desired thickness of embroidered line and select yarn accordingly. For example, if the sock was knitted with a 2-ply yarn but you'd like a bolder line, double the yarn for embroidering. Thread a tapestry needle with the yarn.

There are two easy stitches used in the Varsity Sox: Running Stitch and Satin Stitch. These can be combined to make any lettering desired.

Running Stitch (to left in illustration) creates a simple line that can stand alone or support the Satin Stitch (right) for more drama.

For Running Stitch, simply insert tapestry needle up from underside of knitting at A, down into knitting at B and back up at C, which is approx half-way between A and B.

Tip: If creating curving lines or mock-cursive lettering, use short stitches so the overlapping stays tidy (see center example in illustration).

The example at right in the illustration shows the Satin Stitch being worked over a foundation of parallel lines of Running Stitch that help support the Satin Stitch while keeping the knitted fabric gauge intact. To work Satin Stitch, insert the tapestry needle down at D and back up at E.

BEADED SWEET VALENTINE

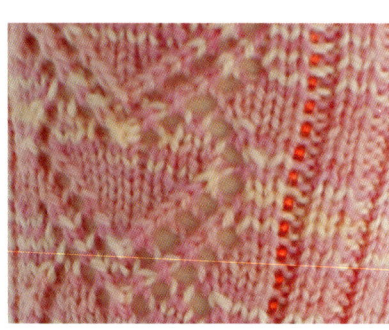

As a bonus, here is a beaded variation of February's Sweet Valentine. You will additionally need 224 size 8/0 (3 mm) beads. The pictured model uses Miyuki 8/0 (3mm) seed beads, 7g Silver-lined Red #10 to suggest red-heart hard candies.

Refer to January's Renaissance for general instructions about stringing beads and bead knitting terms.

For each Beaded Sweet Valentine sock, string 112 beads. Follow instructions as for Sweet Valentine, except on even-numbered rnds of the Ribbing and Hearts Panel, do the following: *(k2, p2) 3 times, k2, sl bead-pl, k15, sl bead-p1*

HEARTH & TREE ORNAMENT

Cast on 42 sts. Join, placing mkr for eor.

Work **Cabled Ribbing** rnds 1 – 4 twice, then rnds 1 – 2 once more for 10 rnds total.

Work **Wreath Cable** rnds 1 – 17 only.

Next 2 rnds: k3, p3, k3, p2, k2, p2, k3, p3, k21.

Reposition eor to side of sock: remove mkr, k3, p3, k3, p2, k2, p2, k3, p3, k2, replace mkr.

Setup for 21 st heel: (k1, sl 1) 5 times, m1, (sl 1, k1) 5 times.

Place remaining 22 sts on hold for instep.

Work Round Heel to depth of ¾". Staying in established pattern on instep sts, dec gussets to 38 total foot sts.

Continue foot in established pattern until sock measures approximately 2" from back of heel.

Work Spiral Toe.

For Hanging Loop, work as for the Hearth & Tree Stocking until cord measures 1½".